Python Data Analytics

Analytics

Programming Language Project

Table of Contents

Introduction

Congratulations on purchasing *Python Data Analytics*
and thank you for doing so.

The following chapters will discuss all of the different
pieces of the puzzle that we need to take a look at and
understand before we can complete the process of data
analytics, and understand all of the predictions and
insights that are found inside that data. Many
companies are already in the habit of collecting large
amounts of data from so many sources, but now it is
time to learn the steps that are needed to put this data
to work to grow your business, make better products,
and serve the customers better than ever before.

The beginning of this guidebook is going to start out
with some information on what data analysis is all
about. We will look at some of the life cycles that come
with data analysis, how to start performing one, and
some of the benefits that many companies and
industries are able to get out of using this process for
themselves. In addition to learning about the data
analysis and some of the steps that come with it, we
will move on to look at what big data is all about, and

how it can become a critical component to everything that we will discuss.

With this information that we now are aware of, it is time to move on to some of the more technical aspects of data analysis, and how we are able to take that data and actually learn what is inside. We will start this part by taking a look at what Python is about, how to do some coding with this language, and the benefits of choosing this coding language over some of the other options that are available. We will also take a quick look at some of the best data science libraries that are compatible with Python that can help us to form algorithms and models in the process as well.

And this leads us into some of the discussions that we will have in the next part of this guidebook. We are going to explore in detail how we can work with a variety of Python libraries to handle all of our data science needs. Some of the libraries that we are going to spend some time on include NumPy, Pandas, Matplotlib, and Scikit-Learn to name a few. Each of these can bring something different to the table when it comes to coding in Python for data analytics, and they are definitely worth our time to become more familiar with and to learn how to use.

The end of this guidebook will give us some of the codes that we want to work with to do some of these data analytics with Python, and then will provide us some of the tips and suggestions that will make this process easier, and will ensure that we are able to use the data to get the results that we need out of that data.

There is so much that we can do with all of the Big Data that is collected and using some of the different libraries and codes that we will talk about in this guidebook, you will be able to analyze your data and find the predictions and insights that you need. When you are ready to get started with data science and with your own data analytics with the help of the Python coding language, make sure to check out this guidebook to get started.

There are plenty of books on this subject on the market, thanks again for choosing this one! Every effort was made to ensure it is full of as much useful information as possible, please enjoy!

Chapter 1: What is Data Analytics All About?

When it comes to data science, there are a lot of different parts that have to come together and work well in order for the business to see the results that they are hoping for. This is a complex process that does not just happen, one that takes some time and effort to finally get the results. If you are hoping to get into data science and data analytics without putting in the work, then this may not be the addiction that your business needs.

With data science, we have a few important steps. We need to collect the data, usually from several sources to make sure that we get the quality and quantity of data that we want. Since the data is coming from more than one source, we need to be able to clean off that data and organize it, putting it in the same format and dealing with any missing values or duplicates. Then we need to analyze the data, usually by coming up with a model or an algorithm that will be able to sort through the information and give us some good results. And finally, it is also important to visualize that data, such as with a chart or a graph, so we can see the insights and predictions at a glance.

All of these parts are important when it comes to the data that we can collect and use to make predictions, help our business grow, and even make our customers happier. We are going to focus mainly on the process of data analytics here, but you will find that in the process, some of the other steps are going to show up because it is all intertwined together. With this in mind, let us explore a bit more about data science and how we are able to use it to benefit and grow our own businesses.

What is Data Analytics?

To start with, we need to have a quick exploration of what data analytics is all about. Data analytics is seen as the science of taking some of the raw data that we have collected or can begin collecting now and analyzing it in order to make some conclusions based on that information. Many of the different processes and techniques that come with data analytics have been automated so they can be done with the right algorithm or mechanical processes. This makes things easier because we can just put that algorithm onto the data, and get some results that we can then look over and base our business decisions on it.

If you use data analytics in the right manner and work to pick out the right algorithm, you will find that these techniques can reveal some metrics and trends that could easily get lost in all of that information. Data analytics works with the idea of big data, which is all of the information and data points that a business collects over time. While it is possible for someone to attempt to go through all of this information, it is definitely not practical.

There are often hundreds of thousands, and sometimes more, data points that come into a company all of the time. And this information is not static. We have this information coming in all of the time, causing us to update and see new insights. If you had an employee, or even several employees dealing with this information, it would just take too long for them to sort through it all. By the time they started to make headway on the first bit of the data, there would be several more behind them, and their trends and insights would never be up to date at all and it would not be worth your time.

Data analytics, along with some of the algorithms that you are able to use with it, can help to solve this problem. The right algorithm and model is able to take all of the data that we have available, and turn it into something that we can actually use. And then, when this information is sorted through and ready, we can use it to help optimize some of the processes that occur in our business, while helping increase the overall efficiency that happens with a system inside of our business as well.

Understanding Data Analytics

When we are talking about data analytics, we have to understand that this is actually a pretty broad term and is going to cover a few different things, rather than just one-step of the process. Usually when a business or an individual talks about data analytics, they are going to include all of the steps that come with dealing with data, from gathering it to analyzing it all the way to making visualizations so that others can understand the predictions and insights found in that data.

Data analytics is going to encompass a lot of diverse types of data analysis that you would like to complete. Any type of information that your business gathers can be subjected to the techniques that we find with data analytics. The overall goal here is not to just mess around with the data because we can. It is to help us take that data, usually a large amount of data, and get insights that we can then use to improve things in our business. As a business, you have to decide what processes need to be improved overall, and then you can complete the data analysis to help with this.

For example, one industry that likes to work with data analytics in the manufacturing world. They can use this kind of process to record the runtime, the downtime, and the work queue for the different machines that help them get things done, and then they can go through and analyze the data to plan their workloads better, allowing the machines to operate in a manner that is closer to their peak capacity.

This is going to help the company to be more efficient. They can stop some of the lulls that are showing up in production, ensuring that the machines keep running at the right times and they are not wasting time trying to get the next load going. They can even use the data analysis to make a prediction on when a part is likely to fail and then can schedule maintenance at times that won't affect production, such as at night.

Data analytics can do so much more than just show us how to find the bottlenecks that will show up in production though. Gaming companies, for example, are able to use data analytics to set reward schedules for their players. The point of doing this is to make sure that they can keep a lot of the players' active inside the game, increasing their customer satisfaction and their revenue at the same time. Content companies can also come into the scene and might use many of the same kinds of data analytics to keep customers clicking, watching, or even re-organizing the content in order to gather another click or another view, which helps to increase their revenue.

With this in mind, we can take a look at the steps that are involved in data analysis. No matter what kind of data you are trying to collect, or what you hope to gather out of that information, there are going to be a few steps that come into play to help us really gather up the data and see some results. Some of the steps that you need to follow when you go through the process of data analysis will be.

The first thing that we need to take a look at here is to figure out the requirements that you would like to put on the data, or how you would like to see the data grouped. There are a lot of options that come into play with this one, and sometimes you may choose to separate out the data based on the income, the demographics of the customer, the age of your customer, and the gender. These are just a few examples of what you can do with all of that data, and how you can turn it into something that is beneficial for your needs.

In addition, some of the data that you gather could be numerical. This helps you to sort out the information based on the number that comes with it. Some

15

companies have more categorical data, where they can search through the information and divide it up into a few categories to help them see the insights and the predictions a bit more clearly.

The second step that we are able to follow, once we know some of the requirements we have for our data is to start collecting it. Often this takes us a bit to go through because we can collect this information form a lot of different sources to help us out. Companies will find that there are many sources they can use in order to gather up the data, such as online sources, cameras, computers, social media, environmental sources and more.

You have to decide early on, where you would like to be able to gather all of this information. This can go back to the business requirements that you worked on before. You need to decide what you are going to use the data for, and then collect the data from the sources where it is going to meet those requirements. You probably do not need to gather the information from all of the different sources that are out there, which can save you time and a lot of money in the process.

Knowing exactly where the information that you need is located and where to collect it from can be a lifesaver in the process.

Once we have had some time to collect the data, which can take a while based on what kind of information you are collecting and how much of it you would like to hold onto, it is time to move on to the third step of organizing the data. We are not able to learn what is inside the data or analyze it in an effective manner if we are not able to organize it at all.

There are a few steps that we are able to use in order to organize some of the data that we have. For example, this organization can take place on a spreadsheet sometimes, or a company may choose to use some form of software that is able to handle the statistical data and make sure it is in a format that we are easily able to look through and understand.

From here, we get to the step of cleaning the information and data off before we work on our analysis. Because you are getting the data from many different sources, you have to make sure that you have it cleaned and ready to go. This ensures that the data is going to work with the algorithm that you set and makes it easier overall to see some good results in the process as well.

What we mean by cleaning up the data before the analysis is that we are going to scrub it and check it out to ensure that inside the data, we are not dealing with errors or duplication and that the information has all of the values in place and nothing missing in the process. This is a good step to spend some time on because it helps us correct any of the errors that are there before we send over the data to our data scientist to analyze it for us.

With this in mind, there are a few key points that we need to reiterate to make sure that we fully understand what is going on with the data analysis, and why it is as beneficial to our company as a whole. The key takeaways for this part will include:

1. Data analytics is simply the process or the science of taking raw data and then analyzing it in order to form some good conclusions about all of the information.

2. The various processes and techniques that come with data analytics are often going to be automated into a more mechanical process. The algorithms can help take all of that data, no matter how much there is, and turn it into a form that humans can consume.
3. The process of data analytics is important to use because it can help business any time they would like to see some optimization in their performance.

Why Does Data Analytics Matter?

Data analytics is going to be so important in almost any industry because it is going to be one of the best and most effective ways that a business is able to optimize the way they perform. Implementing data science and data analytics into your model for business means that you can reduce costs by finding some new and more efficient methods of doing business, and by storing large amounts of data at the same time.

There are many reasons that a company is going to choose to add in some data analytics to the mix, and you can choose which reason or motivation is the best for you. For example, companies like to work with data analytics to help them make better decisions for their business. Others like to use data analytics to analyze the trends and satisfaction of their customers over time. And more, others enjoy using it to help them come up with new and often better products and services to offer.

The Different Types of Data Analytics

There are also a few different types of data analytics that you are able to work with, based on your needs and what you hope to get out of the process. For the most part, and to keep things simple, we are going to break the process of data analytics into four basic types. These will include:

1. Descriptive analytics. This is the kind of analytics that you will use to describe what has been shown over a period of time. A few examples of what you may find here, or look for here include whether the sales are stronger this year than they were at the same time last year or has your number of views gone up online?
2. Diagnostic analytics. This one is a bit different because it is going to focus some more on why something happened the way that it did. This one

is going to involve more diverse inputs of the data, and you will need to bring in your thinking cap to make a good hypothesis here. For this one, you would want to look at something like how the weather affected the sale of beer or another product that you sell. Alternatively, you can look to see how the latest marketing campaign that you sent out helped or hindered your sales for that time period.

3. Predictive analytics. This type of analytics is going to help us figure out what is most likely to happen in the near term. It will not focus as much on the long term but can help us with some of the predictions that will not go too far in the future. For example, you may use this to figure out how your sales did the last time the summer was really hot and then look to see how many weather models out there are predicting another hot summer.

4. Prescriptive analytics. This one is going to help us figure out the best course of action. So, looking back at the hot summer, if you see that the likelihood of a hot summer is measured as an average of five weather models and it is more than 58 percent likely, then you would change up the sales that you do and even the shifts and hours, to handle the increase that you are likely to receive here.

The neat thing with data analytics is that it is going to underpin some of the quality control systems that happen in many industries, but especially with the financial world. We often see data analytics come into play with other business improving measures, like Six Sigma. Six Sigma is all about improving the efficiency of a business and reducing waste, as much as possible, and data analytics is definitely a big part of this.

The idea of Six Sigma and data analytics combining is that if you aren't measuring something in the proper way, whether it is the amount you weigh or how many defects show up in your product per million in the production line, it is pretty much impossible for you to find a way to optimize this. And data analytics helps you to know this information and figure out the best process for optimization along the way.

Who Is Using Data Analytics

Now that we have had some time to discuss data analytics and all of the different parts that come with it, it is time to get a good look at who is actually using this information and how they are benefiting from gathering the data, storing it, cleaning and organizing it, analyzing it, and doing some visualizations on the data as well. This is not just a theory we are talking about. It is actually something that many businesses are using to help them gain a competitive edge and reach their customers a bit better.

One example of an industry that is going to benefit from using data analytics will include the travel and the hospitality industry. We know that these industries are constantly busy and need to make sure that the turnarounds that they offer are as quick as possible. This is how they make sure that they can serve the customers quickly, and make as much money as possible, whether it is a peak season at the time or not.

The travel and hospitality industry is able to use data analytics by collecting customer data and then reading through it, with the help of a model or a few algorithms. Then, with the help of all these tools, they are going to learn where the problems in their business or industry are if there are any, and then come up with the most efficient and the fastest methods of dealing with all of those issues to help improve profits.

Another industry that can benefit from the use of data analytics in healthcare. This is going to combine the use of high volumes of data, and this data can be unstructured or structured and uses the process of data analytics to help those in this industry to make decisions that are fast and efficient. As this progress, it can help doctors to do their job more efficiently, can lessen the workload, and could help save lives.

The retail industry may not be one of the places that you think about first when it comes to data science and data analytics, but there is a lot to love here as well. Think about all of the data that stores and shops are able to gather on their customers, and if the company is smart, they can use all of this information to meet the ever-changing demands of shoppers. The information that these retailers are able to collect, and then follow through with analyzing, will help them to identify trends, provide recommendations on products, and see an increase in profits.

These are just a few of the examples of what we can see when industries and companies see the value in data science and what data analysis is able to do for them. It opens up a lot of possibilities that they may not have considered before and can make it so much easier to see what the customer wants, how to pick out the best products to develop, how to become more efficient, and increase their bottom line.

There is so much that we are able to do when it comes to data analytics. Many companies are already collecting a large amount of information to use. But just gathering the information and letting it sit there, without actually analyzing it and seeing what insights are there is a complete waste of time. You may as well not do any data gathering in the first place.

Having someone manually go through the data does not make much sense either. This is going to take too long to accomplish, and by the time you receive any results at all, the information is not up to date and not worth your time. This is an old practice that we do not need to spend our time on any longer because data analytics can come right in and get it all done for us in no time.

Data analytics can take all of that information, and it is likely that you have a ton of information you are holding onto and can sort through it and find the insights and the important information in no time at all. Depending on what your business goals are, and what information you are trying to extract out of the data, you will find that the data analytics is the best option to pick out the algorithm you want to use and get results.

Almost any business and industry are able to benefit from doing some of this data analytics, and as we go through this guidebook some more, we will start to see some of the other ways that we can use data analytics, and some of the libraries and coding languages that you can use with this as well. Do not let this scare you though. We will work with the Python language, some of the great Python libraries are going to make this process so much easier, and it will not take long before you write out some of the algorithms that you need to see results with your data analysis. With this in mind, let us dive in and see what cool things we are able to do with the help of Python and the process of data analytics to help us out.

Chapter 2: Why Are Companies So Interested in Data Analytics?

When you took some time to read the last chapter, it is likely that you noticed a lot of benefits that can come out of performing one of these data analysis. It is actually something that can benefit many different businesses and industries, and the way that it is going to provide some benefit to you will depend on what your overall goals are. When the analysis is done in the right way, you will be able to see that it can help you to improve customer relationships, pick out the right products that you want to develop and bring to market, reduce waste while increasing the amount of efficiency that is happening, and beat out the competition.

There are a lot of benefits that come with using this process of data analysis, and that is what we are going to spend some time discussing in this chapter. At times, it is easy for a business owner and others looking at data science to get a bit excited. They may think that the data itself is boring, but they know when they use the data in the right manner, and they pick out a good algorithm or model to use with the data, they are going to get some amazing results in the process. They will get insights that they may never have thought about in the past, which can help to propel them into the future.

At this point, it should be obvious that by taking all of that data that you have collected over time and then analyzing it will provide you with a bunch of strategic benefits. Business Intelligence tools are going to bring companies a lot of information and insights about their own company, and about the industry that surrounds them, that they previously knew nothing about. And this is something that is prevalent in most mid and large-sized companies around the world.

It is amazing what we do not know about our business and our customers. And the modern world of commerce makes it almost impossible to keep up with all of this information and to understand what everyone wants. A data analysis can come in and take all of that data that we have collected, and let us know some of the unknowns, which leads us to some better business decisions, ones that are backed by a lot of data and proof, rather than ones that we just guess on or follow our intuition with.

The Benefits of Data Analysis

Now it is time to take a look at some of the benefits that we are going to see when it comes to doing data analysis. There are so many reasons why companies are jumping on board with this, and why so many others are at least taking a look to see what is there and whether or not it is a good idea for them. Some of the benefits that your company may be interested in, and some of the reasons why you should consider going with data analysis will include:

The first benefit that we will see with data analysis is that it will provide your company with access to a lot of tools, ones that help with statistics and other options for reporting. These tools come together to help us find some of the hidden data, the kind that is driving change and growth in an organization, but also the kind that is not going to be measured that often.

We will also find that a good data analysis is going to provide us with one single point of view into data that is pretty diverse. This is going to happen through the implementation of data mining, as well as some other techniques that help out with data farming. While it is at it, this analysis is going to help us to identify some of the value measurements that may not be seen as traditional, which means that they are often overlooked. Just because these are overlooked and non-traditional does not mean that we are not going to be able to benefit from using them, and these may be the exact ones that we need to look at to find the insights and predictions that we want.

Next on the list is that data analysis is going to create for us the ability to acquire any pertinent data that we need. This pertinent data is going to be based on the decisions we want to make, or our business goals, but the data will be used to help us make quality decisions based on the actual conditions and trends that we see in our business.

Everyone wants to make sure that they are planning things out in their business based on the most effective method of getting it all done. A good data analysis that includes high-quality data is going to be able to provide us with a way to link strategic enterprise data to some of our current business activities, along with connecting it back to some of the planned business activities that we have coming up in the future.

Many companies have found that a good data analysis is able to help them learn more about their customers. This, as long as it is used in a good and ethical way, can really help out both parties. The customer is going to receive specialized services and offers and a better experience with the company. And the company is able to benefit because they can increase customer satisfaction, can help them to choose which products they would like to develop and offer, and overall ensure that they see a positive increase in their profits and bottom line from all the work.

And finally, this analysis is going to help us to gain the kind of intelligence that we need to create an advantage over our competition. A good data analysis, one that takes careful planning and doesn't just hurry through the results will provide us with access to something known as competitive intelligence. This competitive intelligence is going to be there to create a nice competitive advantage in all that we do. And when we combine this with the fact that the data analysis is able to help us not only track, but also measure our Key Performance Indicators, you can see how this is beneficial in more than one manner.

More About the Data Analysis

The most effective decision support systems are going to rely on the ability of the management to really understand and follow the underlying data that the company is holding onto. If the management does not understand how this works for some reason, whether they are not looking at the data or are not allowed to follow through with it, then this can lead to some problems with the process of data analysis.

Key businesses activities, including those for human resources management and planning, financial planning, sales and marketing activities, and any of the other activities from other key departments are going to see a big improvement when the key decision-makers can actually gain access to all of the tools that they need, and the ones deemed necessary, to finish up with a complete and strategic data analysis. Without this, then all of that data and information is just sitting around useless and not being used for anything that can help the company.

The gap that is there between the ability to link the performance of the business with the strategic data is something that technology is trying to bridge. This is being delivered in the form of BI tool providers, or Business Intelligence tool providers, including Business Objects, Oracle, and Microsoft to name a few of the options.

One example of this is from Microsoft. The suite of BI tools that this company offers can be an added advantage because it recognizes that all businesses are going to have different needs when it comes to using BI. The suite of BI tools offered from Microsoft is able to scale up or down to fit the needs of all users, whether they are technical or not, in businesses of all shapes and sizes. These tools are going to be completely compatible with the Microsoft line of database products of course, along with some of the database products that come with SAP and some other manufacturers.

This is just one of the options that you are able to use when it comes to data science, and with all of the options and the benefits that we talked about above, it is likely that you see now why so many companies are jumping on board when it comes to data science and performing a data analysis to help them see some big improvements.

Any industry out there, whether they are small, medium or large will be able to benefit from using data analytics, as long as they are willing to put in the time and the work, and actually use the insights that come out of the process, rather than making up their own guesses and assumptions in the process. With the right tools and the right models and algorithms, you can get the data analysis to provide you with all of the benefits that we listed out above.

Chapter 3: An Introduction to Big Data and Which Industries are Benefiting from It?

While we are on the topic of data science and data analysis, we need to take some time to also talk about what Big data is all about. This is a unique term that we need to pay attention to on for a bit now, in order to help us learn more about how a company is able to use this data, and why it is so critical to the data analysis process.

To start with, big data is going to be a term that can help us describe a very large volume of data. A company usually spends a good deal of time looking for and then storing the data, and it can be found in both the unstructured and the structured format. We have to remember here that while Big Data usually talks about a large amount of data, the size of the data or the amount of data that a company has control over is not the most important thing. Instead, what the company decides to do with all of the data they hold onto is going to be the most important.

You can store millions of points of data for years on end if you want to. But if it is just sitting in cloud storage or another location, and you never search through it or analyze it, then the data is worthless. This is where the data analysis is going to come into play. This analysis will ensure that we can actually take all of that data, and instead of leaving it all in storage, it helps you to look through the data to find predictions and insights that lead a company to make smart business moves and decisions.

Why is Big Data So *Important?*

The first thing that we need to take a look at here is why this big data is going to be so important? Why are businesses all over trying to gather this data in the first place and how are they supposed to analyze it to find some of the most important information that is inside.

Remember from before that big data isn't really going to revolve just around how much data you hold onto. Sure, having more data can help with this process because it opens up the door to more information. But the most important thing that we need to keep track of here is what we do with the data, regardless of how much we have.

As a business, you are able to take the data that you want to use from any source, and then analyze all of that information to find some answers that help your business to improve in so many ways. Businesses have been able to analyze big data to help them find the best places to reduce their costs, to reduce the amount of time it takes to do certain processes, to help optimize the offerings that they give to customers and with the development of new products, and to ensure that everyone in the business who makes decisions choose the best path for helping the business grow.

When you are able to do the data analysis, and combine the Big Data together with some of the high powered analytics that we will be able to get with Python in a bit, there is a lot of business-related tasks that someone will be able to accomplish in the process. Some of the tasks that you can do when all of this comes together will include:

1. Helping financial institutions and other companies detect fraudulent behaviors before the activities get so far that it starts to affect your business.
2. It can help you to look through a risk portfolio and then recalculate this whole thing in a few minutes rather than taking days or weeks like those that it did in the past.
3. Can reach your customers right at the point of the sale, and will generate coupons for the customer to use. The types of coupons that are used are going to be based on the kind of buying habits that the customer has had over time.
4. Can help us to determine some of the root causes for something failing. It can also help to figure out some of the defects and other issues of sins near real-time.

The Current Considerations of Big Data

The next thing that we need to take a look at is some of the considerations or the parts that make up the big data that so many companies are so interested in today. We have to remember that the whole term of big data is still new and growing, but the whole process of gathering and then storing up lots of data and then analyzing that information at some point is something that companies have been doing for a very long time.

One of the best definitions that can help us understand more about Big Data comes to us from an industry analyst in the early 2002, known as Dough Laney. His ideas brought us what is known as the three V's of data science and of big data, which help us to see what all of this is about.

The first V is going to be volume. We can imagine that most companies who want to work with data analysis will want to collect a lot of data to help them find their predictions and insights, and often they want to collect all of this data from a lot of different sources. We may find this volume of data from a variety of sources like social media, surveys, transactions that happen with the business, machine-to-machine data, and even from some sensor activity.

The second thing that we need to take a look at is the velocity. Data right now is able to stream in at us at a speed that we could not have imagined just a short time before. Even with the amount of speed that we are seeing all of this data come in, we still need to be able to deal with the data in a manner that is timely and easy to work with. Smart metering, sensors, and other methods are coming in to help us deal with all of the data that is coming in, and many of these are able to keep up in near real-time.

Then the third V that we need to concentrate on here is going to be the Variety. Data is going to head our way from all different types of formats. This is one of the best ways to gather data because it allows us a lot of variety and ensures that the data makes sense for our needs as well. We are going to receive some data that is more structured, including data that is numerical and from databases that are more traditional. Then we can get ahold of data that is unstructured as well. This is going to include some text documents, emails, audio, financial transactions, and even videos.

We can take this even a bit further and add in a 4 V and a C to make this come to a close and to get an even better idea of what we are going to see with Big Data. The Other V that we are going to explore here is the variability. In addition to the increasing varieties and the velocities that come with our data, data flows are things that are a little bit inconsistent. There will be times when we see a peak in the flow of the information, and other times we are going to see this information flow go down.

This is perfectly normal for most businesses, but learning when these things are happening and what is causing them can make it easier to prepare and see results in the process as well. You can look at what event is triggering these peaks and then work to manage this challenge as much as you can.

And the final piece of the puzzle that we need to add in here is the complexity. As you look over all of the places where you are able to gather your data, you will see that it comes from a variety of sources. This sometimes makes it hard for the data scientist to come in and match, cleanse, and later transform the data across many systems. However, it is necessary for us to connect, and then correlate, the multiple data linkages, hierarchies, and relationships. We need to keep up with all of this though, no matter how complex it may seem, otherwise we are going to end up with data that is spiraling out of control.

Who Will Use the Big Data?

The next piece that we need to explore a bit is which companies and industries are the most likely to use Big Data? It is likely that any and every industry out there can benefit in some way from using Big Data, but some are jumping on early because they see the benefits right away. Big Data is something that has an effect on all companies and pretty much all industries. Some of the industries that we can explore now to see how they already benefit from Big Data will include:

The world of banking is first on our list. Think about all of the data that a financial institution or a bank is seeing on a daily basis. Between the transactions in your account, loans that are offered, payments, and more, it is a ton of data that needs to be guarded and protected. You would not be very happy if your bank account was suddenly drained dry and you could not get the money, or someone just handed out your bank account number.

These are some of the things that a financial institution has to spend their time solving, and Big Data, as well as data analysis, will be able to help. This industry will use this process to understand their customers, boost the amount of satisfaction that their customers have in them, minimize their risks, cut down on fraud, and ensuring that they remain in compliance with any and all regulations on the industry.

Then there is the government and the various agencies that fall under this category. These government agencies are going to harness and then apply analytics to the big data that they gather and this allows them to gain a lot of ground. These agencies are going to be able t use big data to help them manage utilities, run their agencies properly, prevent crime, and deal with the problem of traffic congestion. And these are just the starting points to help us see how Big Data can make a difference in the government.

The third industry that can benefit from the use of Big data is going to be education. When an educator can arm themselves with insights that are driven by data, it can really make a huge impact on the students, the systems that school sues, and the curriculums that are offered. These educators are able to analyze all of this big data and then identify the students who are the most at risk. This allows them to watch and monitor these students a bit more, help them learn in different ways, and ensure that this student is able to make the best progress possible with the help of the parents, the principals, and the primary teachers in the mix.

Another industry that we need to look at when it comes to using Big Data is the world of healthcare. There is so much information that comes through the industry of healthcare, and things need to be handled in a timely manner, or as quickly as possible. At the same time, this information needs to be guarded and protected so that not just anyone can see it, and those in this industry are held up to some stringent industry regulations and a high level of transparency.

Big data is able to help with all of this. It can help us to get work done quickly, while also protecting the information of the patients the whole time. In addition, when it is managed in an effective manner big data is able to help health care professionals, no matter where they are, to uncover some of the hidden insights that they need to help provide the best in patient care.

We can also look at how the world of manufacturing is going to benefit from using these Big data. When manufacturers can arm themselves with the insights that we get from big data, they are able to do a bunch of things. Many companies who have started to use this process are able to see two main benefits at the same time. They will be able to minimize the amount of waste that they see while boosting the quality and the output that they can provide. Both of these are key processes when it comes to the highly competitive market that is out there.

Because of all these benefits, and the proof that nothing else can provide them in the same way that data science and Big Data can, many manufacturers are working in a culture that is analytics-based. What this means is that they are able to solve any of their problems in a faster method, while making all of their business decisions more agile.

And the final industry that we are going to take a look at here that is able to benefit from using Big Data is the industry of Retail. When it comes to the retail industry, and all of the different options and competition out there, being able to build up strong relationships with the customer is critical to seeing success. And the best way to help manage these relationships is going to be with some management of big data.

With this in mind, retailers need to know the best way that they are able to market to their customers. They can also use this to help them figure out the most effective methods they can use to handle any transaction that comes in and the most strategic way to make sure that they can bring back any business that has lapsed. And when it comes to dealing with all of these issues and more, all of which are really important to seeing success in the retail industry, Big Data is going to be the heart of getting it all done.

Making Decisions About Your Big Data

We also need to take a look at some of the decisions that we need to make when it comes to using big data. There are three main decisions that we need to make here after we have been able to collect all of that data and these decisions will include:

1. How to store and then manage your data. You need to decide where you would like to store the data. This is something that you may have struggled with in the past, but now there are a lot of options that you can use that can hold onto a lot of data, while keeping your costs low. Pick out a good storage place for your data that will help you keep it until you are ready to do an analysis.
2. How much of the data to analyze. This is going to depend on your needs and what you plan to accomplish. Some companies are going to analyze just some of the information based on their business question, and some will analyze all of it. You can always look through some of the data upfront to figure out what parts of the data are the most relevant before you can analyze it.
3. How to use the insights and the predictions that you are able to find. The good news here is that the more knowledge you have, the more confident you will be in making some of the decisions for your business. It is always a good idea to have a strategy in place so that you can handle the information once you learn and the insights that you are able to garner from all of this.

All of these decisions are important in helping you get started with some of your Big Data. This data is so useful when it comes to helping you learn more about your industry and what you want to do against the competition. When you follow these steps and really understand all that is possible with data science, you are more likely to see some amazing results in the process that help out your business.

Where to Get Your Big Data

The next thing that we need to consider as we go through this process is where we can get our Big data. The good news is that there are many sources to use in order to find this data, and the location you go in particular is going to depend on what you want to do with it, and what big business questions you would like to have answered.

One place where you can look for this Big Data is from streaming sources. This is going to include data that is able to reach your IT systems from a web of connected devices. We will often find that this is also part of the IoT. You can then analyze this data, right when it arrives at your system if you would like, and then decide what you should keep, what you should get rid of, and what needs you to look it over more and gain a better analysis.

Another source of all this information that you will use in the analysis later is social media data. Data that shows up with social interactions is becoming even more attractive, especially when it comes to some of the various functions of your business like support, marketing, and sales. This kind of data is going to come in the form of unstructured in most cases, so be ready to handle that challenge if you choose to work with it for your own needs.

And the third source of information that you can use to help gather your data is going to be from any source that is publicly available. There is a massive amount of data that you can gather from open data sources, including data.gov, the CIA World Facebook, or the European Union Open Data Portal. Just make sure you check what the original source of that information was before using it , to see if there is any bias or lean for the information that you need to be careful about as you go on.

Big data is going to be so important to the whole process of data analysis and in helping your business to see some big improvements overall. Every business and every industry is going to benefit from using data science to see some results, and collecting the Big data and knowing where it comes from is one of the first steps to doing your analysis and seeing the results that you want.

Chapter 4: Introducing Python and How It Can Work with Data Science

Now that we know a bit more about data analysis and all the benefits that we can get with this process in our business, it is time to take a look at some of the coding that comes with this. In order to do an accurate prediction or analysis of all that data that we have been collecting, we need to actually take some time to create a model, usually one that is written by an algorithm, to help us sort through all of that data.

It is unreasonable to expect that a human would be able to go through all of this information and provide us with the predictions that we need to see things happen. There is just too much data to go through, and it would take too long. By the time they could get through the data, the information would be old and it would not be something that could help out your business.

This is where some of the programming need to come into play. When we are able to take some of the data that we have collected and turn it through a model or use a few algorithms on it, we can easily go through very large amounts of data and find some of the hidden insights and predictions that are there. These models are going to be really fast, and efficient, and can provide near real-time predictions in many cases.

One of the best languages to use with this, and the one that provides the best data science libraries, is going to be Python. If you have spent any time in the world of coding and programming, then you are sure to have heard about Python and some of the things that it can do. And now we are going to spend a bit of our time looking at some of the benefits that come with using this coding language over some of the others, and some of the main reasons why we want to work with it when doing data analysis.

What Is the Python Language?

When it comes to picking out a good coding language that you want to work with, none can provide you the benefits that you are looking for quite like Python. There is just so much to love about this coding language, and while many programmers may have their favorite and not want to work with Python, for those who are brand new to coding and have never done any before, and especially those who are looking to do some work with data science, Python can be one of the best options.

The Python code was designed with the beginner in mind. Traditionally coding languages were hard to learn how to use, and it could take a lot of time and effort in order to figure any of it out. Most of the time, the programming and coding were reserved for those who had spent years learning about it and had a lot of experience with it, and the learning curve was pretty steep. With the help of Python though, a lot of these issues went away because it was designed to work well for those who did not have all of that education and experience, but still wanted to learn how to code.

There are a lot of benefits that come with the Python code, and this is one of the biggest reasons why so many people jumped onto it and want to learn it. This is even more prevalent when it comes to the world of data science because this language is not only easy to learn for a beginner, but it provides all of the power and extensions that are needed to make a coding that much easier, even with something as complex as the process of data science. With this in mind, some of the benefits that we will see when it comes to working with the Python language over other coding languages include:

It is designed for beginners. If you are worried about getting into data science because you think it will be too hard to learn a new language, then Python is the right option for you. You will find that the Python coding language is easy to learn, and it has been designed to use some simple rules, plain English, and other great features that have driven programmers to it for years. You will find that it is easy to catch on to some of the basics of coding in this language, and with a little practice, you will be able to use it for all of the data analysis predictions and insights that you need.

It has enough power to get all of your work done. Even though this is a language that was designed to make coding possible for any programmer, even a beginner, this doesn't mean that we need to sacrifice on the amount of power that we will get out of this language. In fact, you may be surprised at how much power is here! Python is able to handle many tasks, including data analysis, artificial intelligence, and machine learning and is considered one of the best at doing this job. This should give us a good idea of the amount of power we are able to find within this coding language.

It comes with a lot of libraries and extensions to help out. If you cannot get things done with the traditional Python library, you can extend things out and use one of the other libraries that work well too. We are going to spend some time in this guidebook going through a few of the best data science libraries that are available, ones that bring in the graphing, the visualizations, the math, and the science that are needed to really complete the data science life cycle. These are not tasks that we are able to do with the traditional Python library, so being able to add them in later, using some of the examples that we have in the following chapters, will help us get the work done.

Has a big community. Because of the other benefits that we are talking about in this chapter, many coders and programmers throughout the world, whether they are brand new to coding and doing it for the very first time, or they are more advanced and have been doing coding for years, are falling in love with Python. This presents you with a large community of programmers and developers who will share their tips and tricks to make all of this work as well as possible. Beginners can benefit from advice, example codes, and troubleshooting help thanks to this large community.

Can work with other languages. You will find that one of the benefits that work well with Python is that it does work well with some of the other languages that are out there. Considering that some of the machine learning and data science libraries that we will work with also compile in other languages, this is a good thing to know. Python will be compatible with these languages and will help you to get the work done, even if you have to switch between Python and another coding language.

The library that comes with Python is also quite large. You will be able to handle a lot of the different types of coding that you would like to with the help of just the traditional Python library that comes with the program originally. However, you do need to download some other libraries when it is time to do some data science. The good news here is that these libraries are easy to find online, are free, and only take a few minutes to add to Python so adding in these capabilities, as you need them will not be difficult.

Finally, you will enjoy that Python and most of its extensions are open-sourced and free. This means that you can get started with all of your programming needs, even with data science, for free. There are some third parties extensions out there that you can choose to add on, and these do often cost a bit of money to use. But you can certainly get all of the power and features that you would like with Python, all for free if you would like.

With all of the benefits that come with Python, it is no wonder that so many people are jumping on board and are excited to use this language. And when it is combined with some of the capabilities that are present with machine learning and the best data science libraries, you will be able to see the results that you want out of this in no time.

While we will take a look at Python and how it works in a bit, it is important to note that Python is one of the best languages to work with when it comes to machine learning. Python is a simple language, one that is easy enough for beginners to the world of programming to work with. Yet it still has enough power behind it to make sure that you can still get some of the intense codes done that you would like. The language has a large library, works well with other coding languages if you decide to implement them together, and it is easy enough to read, even if you do not have any kind of coding practice or experience in the past.

In this guidebook, the examples that we are going to take a look at are going to work with Python. This is going to be helpful to ensure that you are able to work on any of the codes that you would like, without having to worry about learning something that is too complicated to work with. If you have worked with Python in the past, then this is good news. And even if you have worked with a different kind of coding language in the past, this coding language is easy enough for you to learn and understand very quickly.

How Does Python Work with Data Science?

Now that we know a bit more about the Python and how this coding language is going to work, and some of the benefits of using it, we need to take a moment to explore how data science can benefit from the use of Python being there. Many of the benefits that come with Python really help us to see how data science can see some results in the process, but let us dive into this a bit more to see what we are able to learn.

First, Python is able to bring in all of the power that we need to work with data science, especially when it comes to machine learning. When we start talking about some of the libraries and extensions that go with Python in the next few chapters, you will start to see that Python is powerful enough to run many machine-learning algorithms, which is as critical to working with data science as a whole.

While Python can come into play when it is time to gather the data that you want to use, and it is definitely going to benefit when you need to analyze all of that data. Many of the models and algorithms that you will use to sort through that data and gain your predictions and insights are going to come from machine learning and artificial intelligence. You have the choice to add in any programming language that you want, but the best data science libraries run on Python. And since this coding language is so easy to learn how to use and work with, it makes sense that many businesses are turning to it.

Because Python is so easy to use, while still maintaining a lot of the power that you need to see results, it makes sense that we would turn to it. While you do have the option of other coding languages, if you are a beginner who has never done any coding at all, then you will quickly see why Python is the best option to go with. And when we add in some of the other fun libraries that come with Python, the ones that work with data science and machine learning, you will find that this is the best coding language to get even this complex task done.

Machine learning is a type of artificial intelligence that is going to provide systems with the ability to learn from experience, without being programmed for everything that you need the process to do. Machine learning is going to be concerned with the development of computer applications that can access data and learn from it on themselves.

This kind of learning process can begin with observations or data, like instructions, examples, and direct experience to find the right patterns out of the data, and to use these predictions to know what to do in the future. The main goal that you are going to see with machine learning is that it allows the computer to learn in an automatic manner, without any help or any intervention from humans, and the computer program can make the necessary adjustments as situations change.

When you work with machine learning, you will find that it makes analyzing large quantities of data easier than ever. Machine learning can give us some results that are profitable, but of course, you first have to learn how to set it up, and there are a few resources that are needed before you are able to make this all happen. This type of coding is often going to take a bit more time to work with because you are basically training the models of machine learning to do what you want, even when you aren't there, which can really increase how much the system can do.

One of the things that we can do with the help of Python is use machine learning. Machine learning is going to include a lot of the different models and algorithms that we need to use to teach our systems how to do a variety of tasks. In this case, we are looking at some of the ways that machine learning is able to train the model to handle all of the data that we present to it, and then turn it into a form that we are able to understand. But there are many other tasks that machine learning is able to help us out with including:

1. Voice recognition
2. Facial recognition
3. Search engines. The machine-learning program is going to start learning from the answers that the individual provides, or the queries, and will start to give better answers near the top as time goes on.
4. Recommendations after shopping
5. Going through large amounts of data about finances and customers and making accurate predictions about what the company should do to increase profits and happy customers along the way.

Machine learning is going to show up quite a few times when it comes to working with Python and data analysis, and many of the libraries that we will explore in this guidebook will be able to add on the capabilities that we need in order to complete this analysis. Python on its own may not be able to do much with machine learning. But when we combine it together with some of the libraries that we will talk about in a bit, such as Pandas, NumPy, and Matplotlib, we will find that there is a lot that we can do with the help of the Python language and machine learning.

There are so many things that you are going to love when it comes to using the Python language. Some people are scared about working with data science because they think it is too complicated or they are worried about doing any kind of coding at all. But with the help of Python and the ease of use, along with all of that power, you will be able to create some of your own models and algorithms for analyzing the data and pulling out those big insights in no time at all. And that is exactly what we are going to spend some time on in the rest of this guidebook!

Chapter 5: The Best Python Libraries to Help with Data Analytics

There is a lot that we are able to do when it comes to working with the Python coding language. You can write out some powerful and strong codes along the way, and as a beginner, you will be able to do a lot of the programming and coding that you need. There are a few shortcomings that you will notice when working with the Python library itself, but there are plenty of extensions and more that you can add in, and that will provide you with the power and capabilities that you want with some of your more advanced coding needs along the way.

As you get into the world of data analytics though, there will be a time when you need to work with a model and several algorithms in order to work through all of the data that you have, and then come up with a prediction or the insights that you need. This is often going to be a bit beyond what we can do with the traditional Python library, and we need to add in a few things to make this kind of work happen.

Python allows us a lot of flexibility when it comes to working with different features and on different tasks. The main library that comes with Python when you download it is amazing and is a great place for lots of beginners to start. You will be amazed at all of the tasks that you can complete with just this. However, there are a few tasks that we are not able to complete with the traditional Python library, and this is where some of the libraries we are about to talk about will come into play.

The good news is that there are a number of extensions and libraries that you can add into the system in order to handle the machine learning and the data science that you want to do during this process. These are all going to work with the Python language so you get all of the benefits that come with it, but they add in a few more capabilities that are needed to handle these more complex tasks that are needed for data science to happen.

While we are going to spend some time in this guidebook looking at some of the best data science libraries that work with Python, we are going to start out in this chapter taking a look at some of these, and getting a good idea of why you would like to work with each one. There are a lot of great Python libraries that you can add to the original coding language to really see some great results with a variety of tasks. But some of the best data science or data analytics libraries that work with Python are going to include:

1. Pandas: Panda is a library that is written for Python and can help with data analysis and data manipulation. To be more specific, it is going to offer some data structures and various operations for manipulating any numerical tables you are doing and any time series as well. Pandas is free to download and can help you get a lot of the topics and tasks done that you need to do with data manipulation and data analysis.
2. Statsmodels: This is a module from Python that makes it easier for users to explore the data they have, estimate the statistical models, and to perform statistical tests. You can also get a list that is quite extensive when it comes to descriptive statistics, results in statistics, plotting functions, and statistical tests for different data type and for each of the estimators that you want to work with.
3. Scikit-Learn: This is another open-sourced library that comes with Python. You will find that it is going to feature a lot of different algorithms that

you are able to work with including clustering, regression, and classification. Some of the various algorithms that you are able to work with will include gradient boosting, random forests, Naïve Bayes, logistic regressions, and support vector machines. This library is also designed so that it is going to work well with the scientific and numerical libraries that come with SciPy and NumPy.

4. Mipy: This library is going to be a machine-learning library from Python that has been built on top of the NumPy and SciPy. The GNU scientific library is also going to provide us with a wide range of machine learning methods that can help with a lot of problems that are going to work with unsupervised and supervised learning. This one can work with Python 2 and Python 3.

5. NumPy: This is going to be an open-sourced extension for Python that can help us with a lot of the different processes that we want to be able to solve. This module is going to provide us with some functions that are fast and precompiled and can help out with numerical routines.

   a. We will find that this library is going to help add some support that is needed to handle Python when we want to do large and multi-dimensional matrices and arrays. In addition to this, it is going to supply us with a large library of mathematical functions that are higher in level and are meant to help us operate on all of these arrays.

6. SciPy: This library is going to be the one that is used for all of your technical and scientific computing needs. It comes with modules for a lot of the different tasks that you want to do including signal and image processing, special functions, interpretation, integration, linear algebra, optimization, and some of the other tasks that are common in engineering and science.

7. Matplotlib: This is going to be the extension that comes with NumPy that will help with plotting points for you. It is also going to provide us with an API that is object-oriented so that we can embed the right plots into our applications, with some general-purpose toolkits from GUI, including wxPython.

8. NL TK: This one stand for Natural Language Toolkit and it is going to be more of a suite of libraries and programs that can help with natural language processing. You will find that it is going to come with some sample data and the graphical demonstrations that you need to use while analyzing your data. This library has been used to help as a type of platform for any prototypes and building research systems the way that you want.

9. Theano: This is the library that you are going to work with Python that can help us define, optimize, and then evaluate the mathematical expressions, especially the ones that are going to need to use the multi-dimensional arrays in an efficient manner.

When you are ready to do some work with data analytics and you want to expand out some of the capabilities that come with Python, then the list that we provided above is going to help you to get started. We will take a look at some of these in more detail as we go through this guidebook so you can work to do some of the different parts and see some results in no time.

Chapter 6: The Basics of the NumPy Library

Now that we spent some time exploring what the data analysis is all about, and some of the basic parts that come with it, and we have a better idea of how Python works, and we have taken a look at some summaries of the best data science libraries that you can work with, it is time to take a look at some of these libraries a bit more closely. And the first Python data analytics library that you are able to work with will be NumPy.

To start, NumPy is going to be one of the fundamental packages that you can use for scientific computing with Python. It is often one of the first scientific libraries that programmers are going to download when they want to do any data science or machine learning because it comes with lots of great libraries functions to get your work done. Some of the best things that come with this kind of library include:

1. It has an N-dimensional array object that is really powerful.
2. The broadcasting functions that come with this library are going to be really sophisticated.

3. It also comes with some tools that help us to integrate code in Fortran and C/C++
4. This library is going to also include some other great algorithms and models that you can use including capabilities for random numbers, Fourier transform, and linear algebra.

Besides being designed and geared towards being used in the scientific world, NumPy is also going to be used as a multi-dimensional container that can hold onto a lot of the generic data that we want to take care of later. You can use this library to define some of the arbitrary data types that are available, which allows the NumPy library to seamlessly and speedily integrate with many different types of databases as well.

What is NumPy?

From here, we need to take a look into what is offered with NumPy. This is going to be a numerical library that comes from Python and is open-sourced. This is a library that will also come with matrix data structures and multi-dimensional arrays that can help you to get done with some of the data science. You can utilize this library to help you go through a number of operations that are mathematical, especially on arrays such as routines that are algebraic, statistical, and trigonometric.

One thing that we need to remember with this one is that the NumPy library is going to be an extension of Numarray and Numeric. It will come with many different functions that are able to help with transformations, functions for algebra, and mathematical functions. In addition to all of this, it is able to hold onto the generators that are needed for random numbers. We will also find that NumPy is a kind of wrapper that is around a library that is implemented in C. This is not bad news though because it can be combined together with Python so you will still be able to use this coding language.

NumPy is just one of the libraries that you can choose to work with when doing data analysis. It is going to be a great library that goes along with Python that helps us to store more data with less memory. With some of the different resources, including the array that is multi-dimensional NumPy is going to allow programmers who work with Python to store more data, especially when that data is about numbers, in an efficient manner, unlike what they could do in the past.

Pandas is another coding language that we are going to talk about in a bit. Pandas is a great option to use with data science and some of the other methods that we want to work with, and a lot of the objects that come with this kind of library is going to rely heavily on the objects that come with NumPy. Pandas is also a library that can extend out the features and functions of NumPy, so many times these are installed at the same time.

Installing NumPy is easy, especially if you already have the Python library on your computer. You will want to use a pip to make sure that this is going to install the package that comes with NumPy. The code that you need to get this to happen includes:

pip install numpy

Pandas and NumPy are going to be able to complement one another, and this makes them some of the most important libraries that come with Python.

The Important NumPy Data Types

The next thing that we need to take a look at is some of the data types that you can have with this library. There are also a number of objects that you can work with when it comes to NumPy some of the options will include:

1. The one-dimensional array

This is considered one of the most important objects for this kind of library and it is going to be called the ndarray. All of the items that you try to store in this array are going to be the same type. If you try to store different item types in the same array, then you are going to run into some trouble with what you are doing here, and your array is not going to work. An array will contain a collection of objects. It can be any object that you want, as long as the objects in the same array are the same. You can think of the one-dimensional array as a column or a row of a table that has one or more elements.

2. The multi-dimensional array

Now that we have had a chance to work with the one-dimensional array, we need to take a look at one that is considered multidimensional. This one is going to come in with more than one column. A good way to think about this kind of array is like an Excel Spreadsheet. It is going to have columns and rows. And then each of the columns is going to be one of your dimensions.

There are also a few different other types that you are able to work with in order to help make all of this come together and to ensure that you will be able to put the right types of objects into the array that you are using. Some of the options that come with picking out your objects will include the following:

1. Complex
2. Float
3. Integer. This can be both unsigned and signed.
4. Boolean.

Since it is possible to argue that Python is one of the most widely used languages for programming out there, especially when it comes to some of the things that you are able to do with machine learning, it makes sense that we will want to spend some time on this language and the NumPy library as well. NumPy is going to come in and represent a critical core feature of the toolkit that is available for an engineer when it comes to all of the neural networks that you would like to create, and for many of the other programs that you want to do with machine learning.

By utilizing all of the different resources that come with this Python library, many programmers are able to take all of that big data that they have collected and do a higher-level analysis, especially one that is as efficient and fast as possible. Many companies who are doing data science and the data analysis that we have been talking about so far in this guidebook are going to include the Algorithms that come with this library to help them make the right models to look over their current data.

With this in mind, there are going to be other libraries, and some other tools, including SciPy, that can help with getting all of this done. And we are going to talk about this library and other tools in a moment. But none of those choices are going to be able to address all of the needs and things that the NumPy library is able to help out with. For example, NumPy is the only option out of this that is going to help us address the need for large arrays that are multidimensional and it is the only library that is able to help us handle the matrix numerical storage as well.

As we can see, there is so much that we are able to do with the NumPy library when it comes to doing machine learning and performing some of the data analysis that we want. And many of the other tools and libraries that we are going to discuss in this guidebook will be extensions of or rely on this library, so it is definitely a choice that we should focus our attention on and learn how to use along with Python.

Chapter 7: The Basics of the Matplotlib Python Library

The next type of library that we want to spend our time on is the Matplotlib. This one is going to be the most useful when we are working with creating graphs and other useful features in our coding. This is a step that is often easy to forget all about when we are working with data analytics because we are more interested in reading the results that are found, rather than worrying about the best way to present it. But the matplotlib is going to be a great option to use to help us see some results and help us create some of the charts and graphs that we need for results.

The Importance of Creating Visuals

With the information above in mind, it is time to take a look at some of the benefits of using data visualization, and why so many people like to work with this. While it is possible to do the analysis and more on your own, without having any of the graphs and other visuals to go along, this is often a poor way to make decisions, and does not ensure that you really know what is going on with the data in front of you, or that you will see the full amount of information and trends that are presented. In addition to this, some of the other reasons that data analysts like to work with these kinds of visualizations include:

Working with data visualization is going to be so important when you work on any process that includes data analysis. It helps them to make better decisions. Today more than any other time in history, companies have decided to look at a variety of data tools including data visualizations, in order to ask the right questions and make the best decisions for them. Emerging computer technologies and some user-friendly software programs have made it a bit easier to learn more about your company and to ensure that you are making the best decisions for your business, driven with sound data behind it.

The strong emphasis on things like KPIs, data dashboards, and performance metrics are already showing us the importance of taking all of the data the company has collected and then measuring and monitoring it. Some of the best quantitative information that a business may already be measuring right now, and that they could put to good use after the analysis is going to include the amount of market share the company has, the expenses of each department, the revenue that is received by quarter, and even the units or product that are sold by the company.

The next benefit of working with this kind of data visualization is that it can help to tell us a story with a lot of meaning behind it. Data visualizations, as well as other graphics that are informational, have become a really essential tool when we are looking at some of the work the mainstream media is doing. Data journalism is a field that is on the rise, and many journalists are consistently relying on quality visualization tools to make sure they can tell the stories about what is happening in the world around you.

Because so many of us are going to learn better when we can look at the data and see what is present there, it makes sense that we are going to want to work with this rather than just listing out the information and hoping that it makes sense to someone else. You can definitely include some of this information with the visualization so someone can come in and double-check your work, but having that visualization is going to make things easier, and will ensure that anyone who wants the information is able to find it in just a few minutes.

What Matplotlib is All About

Humans are known to be creatures who like to see things in a visual presentation. We can read things all day, and it is possible that it is going to be confusing or we will not be able to absorb it the way that we would like. But when we see something in a visual form, whether it is a picture or a graph or a chart or something else, then the information can click with us faster and more efficiently than with any other method.

We as humans are going to be able to understand things better when we can actually visualize them. However, the step to presenting analyses, insights or results can sometimes turn into a type of bottleneck. You may not have a good idea of where to start, or you might already have the format that you want in mind. Either way, we can then end up with some questions like "is this the right way to visualize the insights that I want to bring to my audience?" and it is an important question to answer.

Any time that you are working with this kind of plotting library through Python, the first step that we need to do to help answer the question that we have listed above or any other question that we have, is to build up our knowledge. Some of the topics that we should concentrate our efforts on to build up that knowledge will include:

1. We need to know about the anatomy of the plot for Matplotlib. We need to know what a subplot, an Ax, and a figure are all about.
2. We need to know about the plot creation. This is sometimes going to raise up some questions about what module you need exactly, and which one you should import. You often need to choose between pyplot and pylab. Other things to consider here would be how you should go about initializing the figure and the Axes of your plot, and how to use the Jupyter notebook along with this library.
3. The plotting routines are important to know about as well. This could include things like simple ways to plot your data, but it can go to some of the more advanced methods to help you visualize some of the data that you have.

4. Customizations to some of the basic plots. This should have a big focus on things like plot legends, axes labels, text titles, and even the layout of the plot you are using.
5. We need to have some knowledge about clearing, showing, and saving your plots. You want to be able to do a lot of different things when it comes to working with some of the plots that you want to do. You need to be able to show the plot, save one or more of the figures to it, and even how to close it up safely when it is all done.
6. And the last thing that we need to spend some time on is how to customize this library to get it to work the way that we would like.

Creating some of the different parts of the graphs and charts and other visualizations that we would like to work with can make a big difference in how you are able to present some of the data that is available to you. And none of the Python libraries can do the work as well and as efficiently as we are going to see with matplotlib.

Different Types of Visualizations to Work With

There are also a few different types of visualizations that you are able to work with when you bring out the Matplotlib library to help you out. The one that you choose to go with is going to depend on what type of data you are sorting through, and what you are hoping to learn out of all that information as well. Some of the information that you look up, and some of the types of data, are likely to lend themselves best to one type of graph or visualization over the others. Some of the best visualizations that you are able to use along with the matplotlib extension will include:

1. The scatterplot: This is the visualization that is used to find a relationship in all of the bivariate data. Programmers will often use this one to find out if there are correlations present between two variables that are continuous in nature.
2. Histogram: Next on the list is the histogram. This one is going to be used when we want to see the distribution present in the continuous variable. In many cases, it is going to show us the frequency of distribution when working with a single variable inside a univariate analysis.

3. Bar chart: This can go by the name of barplot or a bar chart and it is the one that is used to help us represent data that is categorical with bars that are either horizontal or vertical. It is going to be a general kind of plot that is going to allow us a way to aggregate all of our categorical data based on some function. The default for the function that is used will be the mean, but this can vary based on what you would like to see happen.

4. Pie charts: The pie chart is going to be a type of plot that we can use to help represent the proportion of each category in categorical data. The whole pie is going to be divided up into slices, ones that are going to end up equal to the number of categories that you are splitting the information up into.

5. Countplot: The Countplot is going to be similar to what we are going to see with the bar plot, but we are only going to pass the X-axis and the Y-axis to represent explicitly counting the number of occurrences that show up. Each of the bars that are on this is going to count for each category of species.

6. Boxplot: This particular type of plot is going to be used to help us show the distribution of the variable. The box plot is going to be seen as the more standardized way of displaying the distribution of data based on the five-number summary. And this summary is going to include the minimum, the first quartile, the median, the

third quartile, and the maximum so that we can see what is going on with the data.

7. Heatmap. This one is maybe not going to be shown as much as some of the others when you are working with the matplotlib extension, but it is still one that we are going to take a moment to focus on. This is going to be a Matrix plot that can allow us to plot data as the color encoded matrices. It is going to be used in most cases to find a bit of the multi-collinearity in our set of data.

   a. To help us plot one of these maps, we need to have the data organized into the form of a matrix. Then the heatmap is going to go through this matrix and basically add in some colors to help us know which values belong to different parts. We can then glance at the matrix to see the information, rather than having to read through all of the numbers.

8. Distplot: This visualization is going to come into play to help us see what the distribution is all about with the univariate data that we want to work with.

9. Jointplot: This is another option that we can work with and it is going to be used in many cases to help represent the distribution of one variable in order to match it up with the distribution that we will see with another variable. To help us become more specific with this, this kind of visualization is going to allow the programmer to take two

Distplots and match them up for the bivariate data that we have available.

Each of these graphs or visualizations can be so important to helping you to see some results with your data and can make it so much easier to see relationships and understand what is going on compared to just reading through all of the numbers and the information. You can definitely try to work with your data analysis and present the ideas and the insights that are inside of that data to the key decisions makers without the visualization, but you will have to spend a lot more time explaining the data, and there can be a lot of confusion and annoyance in the process. Knowing which visualization to work with, and creating one that really helps to highlight the information, the insights, and the predictions that are found in all of your data can be so important to the results that you get out of your Big Data.

Chapter 8: Working with the Pandas Library in Data Science

The next type of library that we are going to spend our time on is the Pandas library. This is another great library that we can learn about that helps with a variety of tasks with data science, data analytics, and more. In fact, this is one of those libraries that can connect with others, and get all of the tasks of data science and the data life cycle is done for you.

To get started, Pandas is an acronym that stands for Python Data Analysis Library. With this name, we know that we are going to be working with a product that can really help us get things done. It is designed to help out with data analysis, and it relies on Python so we know we are in the right place. According to the Wikipedia page with Pandas, the name is going to be derived from the term, panel data, which is an econometrics term for multidimensional structured data sets. Either way Pandas is a much easier way to remember the name of this process and the library as a bunch of parts that come together and help us see results in the process.

When it comes to helping us to really analyze the data that we have, Pandas is going to be a big game-changer. This is actually one of the most preferred methods, and many programmers use it, to help with things like data munging and data wrangling, and we can use it for all of the parts that are needed for data analysis. Pandas is also open-sourced and it is free to use so this makes it an even better choice for those who want to handle a data analysis without all of the costs involved.

There are a lot of neat things that can come into play when we talk about the Pandas library. But one of the things that you may enjoy is that it is going to take all of the data that your company has been collecting, no matter what kind of form it is in, and then uses that information to create an object in Python that has columns and rows. This new object in Python is going to be known as a data frame and we can think of it looking similar to a table that shows up in other statistical software. If you have worked with the R programming language, then this object would look similar to a table in there, or imagine it like a table in Excel spreadsheets.

As you can imagine, working with a Python object that looks like a table is going to be much easier to work with. This is especially true when we look at comparing it to a list or a dictionary through for loops or for list comprehension. These are other methods that we can use to handle some of the data in data analysis. And they do work, but they take more time, are more complicated, and don't provide the kind of power that we need.

Installing Pandas On Your Computer

The first thing that we need to take a look at here is how we can install this library on our computer. The setup of this program is not that difficult, but we need to make sure that we get it set up right and that everything is as organized as possible so that we can actually use this library with Python for all of our data analytics needs.

To help us get ahold of the Pandas library and have it work properly, we need to go through the process of installing this library. Before you start though, we need to double-check which version of Python is on your system. Pandas are only going to work with Python 2.7 or higher. If you have a version of Python 3 then you will be fine, but anything that is too low will not be able to support the various capabilities that come with this kind of library.

Once you have checked which version of Python is on your system and do any of the upgrades if needed, we also have to remember that Pandas is going to have a dependency on some other libraries like NumPy, so it will not work without that library and some of its functions present. There is also a dependency on Matplotlib that is optional, but it is good to have it set up with this so that you can finish up any project that you would like here with the right plotting and visualizations.

Because of these dependencies, both required and optional, the easiest way that you can get the Pandas library set up and ready to go is to install it through a package like the Anaconda distribution. This distribution is going to be known as one that can go across platforms and works well for tasks like scientific computing and data analysis.

When you get to the main page to help out with downloading this, you have a few options. You can go with any operating system to install this, so it works well with Linux, OS X, and Windows. You can go through and see that there is an installation present for each of these operating systems so you can just choose the one that works the best for you.

The next thing that we need to look at is the use of Pandas in your Python IDE. The IDE stands for the Integrated Development Environment that we will use in order to complete some of our coding with Python. While you can also work with Spider and Jupyter Notebook inside the Python IDE< we need to remember that the very first library that we should import is going to be the Pandas library. This allows it to come over and get everything set up, and then we can add in some of the other libraries and extensions that we need.

Importing the library means that we will load it into the memory, and then it will be present in that location of the memory for us to work with whenever is the most convenient for us. To help us important this Pandas library, you simply need to use the following code:

```
import pandas as pd
import numpy as np
```

At this time, you will also add in the second part of the code (the part that says "as pd") because it allows you to make some of the commands that you will be using later a little easier. When you add in this part, you can easily access Pandas any time that you want with the command of pd.command and nothing else, and without having to write out pandas.command each time that you would like to do this task.

Also, you will need to take some time when writing out code in Pandas to import the NumPy library as well. This library is able to work very closely with Pandas and is a useful library in Python to help with scientific computing. Many of the tasks that you will want to do in Pandas will need to rely on the NumPy library a little bit, so being prepared and ready to handle that can make life easier. Just import it at the same time because it is likely that you will need that library, and it can be a pain to go back through and try to bring it up later.

At this point, the Pandas library is ready to use. You can go through and explore some of the topics that are available with it, and some of the different features and functions that are found with it. Remember here that we need to use the code above any time that we would like to start up with a new file from Spyder or a Notebook from Jupyter as well so it is a good one to remember.

The Benefits of the Pandas Library

We have already had some time to talk about the Pandas library a bit and some of the other options that are out there for you to use with data science and mathematics. The next question that you may have is why you should choose to go with the Pandas library instead of one of the other choices that are available. There are so many benefits that come with the Pandas library, and it really can help you through pretty much all of the stages of working in Python and with a data analysis so it is worth our time to learn more about.

The first benefit of working with the Pandas library is the data representation. Pandas are going to provide us with forms of data representation that are streamlined. This is going to make it easier for the programmer to come in and analyze and understand the data they are looking at a bit better. When the data representation is in a simple form, it is going to facilitate better results for all of your projects in data science.

Less code writing, while still getting more work done at the same time, can be another benefit that you will see with the Pandas library. This is actually one of the best advantages of using Pandas over another option. What would take at least a few lines, but often way more, in Python without the right support libraries, could be done in just one or two lines when using Pandas. This means that Pandas is going to help shorten up the procedure of handling data for the programmer. With the time that we can save with this, we are then able to focus more attention on the algorithms for data analysis.

Pandas also come with a really extensive set of features. Pandas and its library is really powerful and can provide you with a very large set of commands that are important, and features that are meant to help analyze any data that you are working with. We are able to use Pandas to help us perform a variety of tasks, including filtering the data to certain conditions, segregating or segmenting the data to our preferences, and more based on what we would like to see happen.

Pandas is capable of handling some large sets of data in an efficient manner. When this data library was designed, it was meant to handle really large sets of data in an efficient manner. Pandas are going to help us save a lot of time because we can import a lot of data from many sources very quickly, and still get the results.

Another benefit that we may enjoy when it comes to the Pandas library is that it is going to take our data and make it more customizable and flexible overall. Pandas are going to provide us with a huge feature set to apply on the data that you have, making it easier to customize, edit, and pivot that data based on what you would like to see happen with the data. This is useful because it allows the programmer or the data scientist to mess around with the information until they can bring out the most in the data.

And the final benefit that we can see with Pandas is that it works with the Python language. Along with the other options that we discussed in this guidebook, Pandas is going to work well with the Python coding language. This provides you with some of the extra capabilities and extensions that you are looking for when it is time to use the Python language and see what it can do in the world of data science and data analysis.

Are There Any Disadvantages to Using Pandas?

There are a few negatives that come with this kind of library though, and we need to explore what these are all about as well. It is important to get a good look at these because they will determine how much we use the library, and whether or not the Pandas library is actually the right one for us for the coding needs we have. with this in mind, some of the disadvantages that the programmer should have when it comes to working with the Pandas coding language will include the following:

1. Bad documentation: Without the right kind of documentation in place, or even good documentation, it is going to become really difficult to learn any new library at all. Pandas documentation isn't really going to provide us with a lot of help to understand some of the harder functions that come with this library. This is going to end up slowing down some of the learning that we want to do here. You may need to make some plans around this in order to get your project to act the way that you want.

2. It doesn't do well with matrices that are 3D. This is seen by many programmers to be one of the biggest drawbacks of using this library. If you want to work with a matrix that is 2D or two-dimensional, then Pandas can be a great option to use. But once your goal is to create a 3D matrix, then Pandas is no longer going to be the best choice to work with, and then you have to rely on some other library, like NumPy to make this all work.

3. The syntax is sometimes seen as difficult. While Pandas is a part of the Python family, it is sometimes seen as tedious with the types of syntax that it wants to use. The code syntax that comes with Pandas is going to become very different from what we may be used to in the

Python code. Switching back and forth between the two, and trying to manage the Python code and the Pandas code that you need can often turn into a major challenge.

4. The learning curve is steep. Pandas initially started out with a mild learning slope. And if you are just using some of the basics, then you will find that learning how to work with it is not so bad. But the deeper you decide to go into this library, the harder it becomes, and the steeper the learning slope is going to become. The functionality with this one can start to become confusing and will cause the beginners a few problems. However, this is a great library to learn and if you add in a bit of determination to learn something new, even when it is a challenge, you can overcome it all.

Despite the fact that the Pandas library does come in with a few things that we need to be careful about, and a few disadvantages, the positives are going to outweigh the negatives in this case. Each of the libraries that we have talked about is going to come with some positives and some negatives, and we just have to determine if it is still worth our time to use the library or not. And when it comes to the Pandas library, it is definitely more advantageous to use it rather than not.

When you are looking for an additional feature to add into some of the codings that you are doing with data analysis, do not let some of the limitations that come with Pandas slow you down or make you worry about using this kind of program. Instead, look at all of the positives that come with this kind of library, and all of the immense potential that is stored inside.

Chapter 9: Other Common Libraries for Data Science and Why They Are the Best

In addition to some of the libraries that we talked about above, there are many other Python libraries that work very well with some of the data science and the data analysis that you would want to complete. Learning what these libraries are all about, and how to get them to work on your own data analysis is one of the best ways to ensure that you see some success in the process. With this in mind, let's take a look at a few of the other Python libraries that can take all of that data you have collected and form it into something that you can read and understand while completing data analysis.

Scikit-Learn

The first library that we are going to focus on here is the Scikit-Learn library. This is going to be a program that was developed just a few years ago in 2007, but it has been changed and developed to help us do even more when it comes to the world of artificial intelligence, machine learning, and data science and data analysis.

To start with though, Scikit-Learn is a library that is there to provide us with a lot of supervised and unsupervised learning libraries that will work with Python and ensure that you will be able to actually work with machine learning while doing your data analysis. Machine learning is one of the best ways to work with the various algorithms and models that you need to pull out those insights and actually understand what all of the data that you have contains inside. This database is set up to work with commercial and academic use, and it works really well with the SciPy library that we will talk about in a minute.

The library itself was done all in Python, and then some of the algorithms that you are going to rely on here are going to be written with the help of Cython, in order to make sure that you get the best performance out of them as possible. You will quickly find that the Scikit-learn library is the best one for you to work with when building up some of the models of machine learning that you will need. The good news is that this library is easy to get ahold of and it is open-sourced, so you can start using it when you are ready.

It is likely that when you are looking at this library, the number one thing that you will want to take a look at is some of the features that come with this library. And in truth, there are quite a few features that you need to be aware of right from the start. This is a library that is designed not just for data science, but specifically to handle some of the data analytics that we are talking about in this guidebook. Some of the features that are present with this library and are going to matter the most to us as we perform our own data analysis at this time will include:

1. Supervised models: This library is able to provide you with a lot of different generalized linear models for your needs. This would include things like decision trees, support vector machines, neural networks, lazy methods, naïve Bayes, discriminate analysis, and more.
2. Manifold learning: These can be used in order to depict and even to summarize multi-dimensional data that may seem a bit complex.
3. Datasets: This is going to be where you can test out the datasets that you have, the ones that are for generating datasets with specific properties for investigating model behavior.
4. Cross-validation: This one is going to be helpful when you want to estimate how well the

supervised model you have is going to perform on data that is unseen.

5. Clustering: This is where you are able to group any of the unlabeled data, such as the K-means that we will talk about a bit later.

These are just a few of the benefits and features that we will be able to see when we decide to work with the Scikit-Learn library to help with data science. There is also a lot more that we are able to do to make this program work the way that we want, based on our overall goals and what we hope to gain out of all that information as well.

TensorFlow

Now it is time for us to take a look at another library, known as the TensorFlow library. This is going to be more of a framework that we are able to use along with our data analysis, and it comes to us from Google. If you ever need to add in some deep learning to some of the models and analysis that you are doing, then the TensorFlow library is the right one for your needs. This library is going to rely on graphs about the data flow that we see with numerical computations, and it ensures that a lot of the work that we see with machine learning is easy to do. If you want to get through some complex data and learn what is in there, or even make some good predictions based on that data, then the TensorFlow library is the right one for you.

Programmers who decide to go with the TensorFlow library are going to find that it is able to help them out with many of the different aspects and parts that come with working in data science and on data analysis. This library can come into play to help make the process of gathering up the data, training any of the models that we want to use with machine learning, making the right predictions, and even modifying some of the future results so much easier than before. Since each of these steps is going to be so important when it comes to completing data analysis, it makes sense that we would want to at least get some of the basic knowledge of how TensorFlow works.

This is a library that was developed by Google's Brain team to use on machine learning when you are doing it on a large scale. TensorFlow is going to bring together machine learning and deep learning algorithms and models and it makes them much more useful via a common metaphor. TensorFlow is going to use Python, just like what we say before, and it gives its users a front-end API that can be used when you would like to building applications, with the application being executed to a high-performance C++.

TensorFlow can be used for building, training, and running deep neural networks for image recognition, recurrent neural networks, handwritten digit classification, word embedding, and natural language processing to name a few. There is so much that we are able to do with the TensorFlow library, and it is likely to help us out with many of the things that we need to do with data analysis.

SciPy

The third type of library that we are going to take a look at now is known as the SciPy library. This is going to be another great option that is available through Python and works the best on tasks of technical computing and scientific computing. When you decide to use this particular library, you will find that it is going to be set up to handle many of the common tasks for engineering and science. Some examples of what we are able to do with this particular library include FFT, special functions, interpolation, integration, linear algebra, and optimization.

SciPy often goes along with NumPy and it is best if you are able to download these two Python libraries at the same time. This is because the SciPy library is going to build upon the array object that we are able to find with NumPy, and it is already a part of the stack that comes with NumPy. A few other libraries that belong to this same stack are going to include SymPy, Pandas, and Matplotlib, and it is likely that this list is going to expand out to some of the other scientific computing libraries in the near future.

SciPy has been designed with a family of conferences for users and developers of these tools. There are several versions of this based on which part of the world you are in and all of these can help you to do some of the work that you need with data science while maintaining the regulations that are important to see your business grow.

Right now, SciPy is free to use and open-sourced. There are sponsorship and support for this software by an open community of developers. This gives programmers the best of both worlds. They get to know that they can use a great product and a great scientific and data science library for free, while also knowing that there is someone there who is watching the library, keeping up to date, and debugging the program if that is needed.

Few of the different sub-packages that are available with SciPy. These are useful to know about because they are going to ensure that you get the full capabilities of the SciPy library without having any problems with it. Some of the different sub-packages that you can use along with the SciPy library will include the following:

1. Image manipulation
2. Signal processing
3. Fast Fourier transforms
4. Numerical integration
5. Statistics along with random numbers
6. Optimization of the information and fit
7. Interpolation
8. Linear algebra operation
9. Special function

10. File input and file output

These are just a few of the other libraries that you are able to work with when it comes to performing the tasks that you want in Python data analysis. Being able to use these, and understanding what they bring to the table will definitely help you to get the right insights and the right predictions when it comes to working on your own data analysis.

Chapter 10: Some Python Data Analytics Coding to Help You Get Started

We have spent some time in this guidebook looking at the basics of data analysis, as well as some of the things that we need to know to work with Python, and how to put the two together. We have even taken a look at some of the most common libraries that you are able to work with to make your Python data analysis complete. With this in mind, we are going to spend a bit of time in this chapter explores some of the codings that you can do to actually complete part of the data analysis that you would like, and you can use Python the whole time! Some of the models and algorithms that rely on Python and that we can use to do our data analysis will include:

K-Means Clustering

The first option that we are going to take a look at is known as the K-Means clustering. Clustering is a simple process that is often used in machine learning for data analytics and can help us to divide up many of the points of data that we have, and then see where the group of points is going to be located. You get to choose how many clusters are present, based on what you see in the data or what you want to learn.

For example, you may use this to sort out all of your customers into males and females. In this case, you would have two clusters and when the algorithm goes through all of the data, it will make sure that all of the points fit into one of those two clusters. Or maybe you would like to learn who is the most likely to purchase a certain product, and what age group they fall into. This can help with some of the sales and marketing that you are trying to do. In this case, you may split the data up into four or five clusters instead to see a better idea of where all of your customers are coming from and what ages they are.

The idea that comes with this is that any of the data points or the objects that end up in the same cluster are going to be ones that are closely related to each other but won't share things in common with the other people in the other clusters. This similarity is important because it is going to be the main metric that we are able to use to reflect the strength of the relationship between any two objects we want to look over.

Now, an example of a code that you are able to work with that can collect all of the data that you are using, and provides you with information on which cluster they fit into (you get to be in charge of how many clusters there are for the data to fit into), will include the following:

```
import numpy as np
import matplotlib.pyplot as plt


def d(u, v):
    diff = u - v
    return diff.dot(diff)


def cost(X, R, M):
    cost = 0
    For k in range (Len(M)):
        For n in xrange (Len(X)):
            cost += R[n,k]*d(M[k], X[n])
    return cost

def plot_k_means(X, K, max_iter=20, beta=1.0):
    N, D = X.shape
    M = np.zeros((K, D))
    R = np.ones((N, K)) / K

    # initialize M to random
    for k in xrange(K):
```

```
    M[k] = X[np.random.choice(N)]

grid_width = 5
grid_height = max_iter / grid_width
random_colors = np.random.random((K, 3))
plt.figure()

costs = np.zeros(max_iter)
for i in xrange(max_iter):
    # moved the plot inside the for loop
    colors = R.dot(random_colors)
    plt.subplot(grid_width, grid_height, i+1)
    plt.scatter(X[:,0], X[:,1], c=colors)

    # step 1: determine assignments / resposibilities
    # is this inefficient?
    for k in xrange(K):
        for n in xrange(N):
            R[n,k] = np.exp(-beta*d(M[k], X[n])) / np.sum(
np.exp(-beta*d(M[j], X[n])) for j in xrange(K) )

    # step 2: recalculate means
    for k in xrange(K):
        M[k] = R[:,k].dot(X) / R[:,k].sum()

    costs[i] = cost(X, R, M)
    if i > 0:
        if np.abs(costs[i] - costs[i-1]) < 10e-5:
            break

plt.show()


def main():
    # assume 3 means
    D = 2 # so we can visualize it more easily
    s = 4 # separation so we can control how far apart the means
are
```

```
mu1 = np.array([0, 0])
mu2 = np.array([s, s])
mu3 = np.array([0, s])

N = 900 # number of samples
X = np.zeros((N, D))
X[:300, :] = np.random.randn(300, D) + mu1
X[300:600, :] = np.random.randn(300, D) + mu2
X[600:, :] = np.random.randn(300, D) + mu3

# what does it look like without clustering?
plt.scatter(X[:,0], X[:,1])
plt.show()

K = 3 # luckily, we already know this
plot_k_means(X, K)

# K = 5 # what happens if we choose a "bad" K?
# plot_k_means(X, K, max_iter=30)

# K = 5 # what happens if we change beta?
# plot_k_means(X, K, max_iter=30, beta=0.3)


if __name__ == '__main__':
    main()
```

This may be a long code, but remember that we are pulling out a few different libraries and then asking them to take the data points that we have, usually quite a few points of data at that, and then turn them into a form that we are able to read through and understand. Creating the clusters, and then reading through all of the data in order to determine which cluster each one should fit into is a challenge, but with the help of the code above, you will be able to get it all done in no time.

Creating Our own Neural Networks

The next topic that we are going to take a look at is the idea of a neural network. These are really powerful codes, and it may take some time to learn the best way to deal with them, but when it comes to the amount of power that we can put behind them, and all of the work they can do for our codes, it is no wonder that so many people want to add them into their data analysis, and why they will specifically learn about machine learning and artificial intelligence so they can code in this way.

The neural networks help teach our systems how to think as the human mind does. Through learning and remember past experiences, the program is able to become "smarter" and will make better decisions in a faster and more efficient way as time goes on. These neural networks can be really good at what they do, as long as we have the patients and the time to teach the algorithm how we would like it to behave.

Neural networks are often seen as something useful because they are set up to learn in a manner that is similar to what we see the human brain does, or at least in a manner that is pretty close to it. And this is all done through the computer. However, we have to make sure that we are using the right training procedure from the very beginning in order to see some improvements here. If we feed the algorithm low-quality information or information that isn't going to help it to learn, then we may as well give up now.

The higher the quality of information that you are able to feed into the machine, the better. This helps us to really see the program work the way that we want. With high-quality information, we can ensure that the neural network will give the right predictions and insights and that we will have the system learn what it should do faster than ever before.

There are a lot of different parts that come with creating our own neural networks. But for now, we are going to focus on the code that is needed to help us create one of these. A simple neural network that you can create all on your own, with the help of Python, to go through your data and to learn from it will include the following:

```
import torch
import torch.nn as nn
import torch.nn.functional as F


class Net(nn.Module):

    def __init__(self):
        super(Net, self).__init__()
        # 1 input image channel, 6 output channels, 3x3 square convolution
        # kernel
        self.conv1 = nn.Conv2d(1, 6, 3)
        self.conv2 = nn.Conv2d(6, 16, 3)
        # an affine operation: y = Wx + b
        self.fc1 = nn.Linear(16 * 6 * 6, 120)  # 6*6 from image dimension
        self.fc2 = nn.Linear(120, 84)
        self.fc3 = nn.Linear(84, 10)

    def forward(self, x):
        # Max pooling over a (2, 2) window
        x = F.max_pool2d(F.relu(self.conv1(x)), (2, 2))
        # If the size is a square you can only specify a single number
        x = F.max_pool2d(F.relu(self.conv2(x)), 2)
        x = x.view(-1, self.num_flat_features(x))
        x = F.relu(self.fc1(x))
        x = F.relu(self.fc2(x))
        x = self.fc3(x)
        return x
```

```
def num_flat_features(self, x):
    size = x.size()[1:]  # all dimensions except the batch
dimension
    num_features = 1
    for s in size:
        num_features *= s
    return num_features


net = Net()
print(net)
```

Working with a neural network is often seen as a more advanced form of coding compared to some of the other options that are out there. But as we can see with this example, neural networks are not so bad, but the tasks that they are able to take on for you can really improve your overall coding and what you are able to do with a Python data analysis.

Chapter 11: Tips to See Success with Data Analytics with Python

The first thing that we can take a look at here is going to be some of the tips and suggestions that programmers need to follow any time that they want to perform data analytics and use that information to help propel them forward to seeing some great results. There are a lot of different parts that need to come into play when we are working with any kind of data analytics, but especially when we are working with one that involves Python, and having the right tips and suggestions in place ahead of time can make a world of difference in the success that we are going to see. Some of the tips that you can follow will include:

1. Look at the statistics first

Many programmers are going to get ahead of themselves in the process and will take on an analysis that is more complex before they have even spent some time doing an examination of the data from the most basic of perspectives. Often some of the descriptive statistics that we need to look at first are going to provide us with some critical context that you can use later on for some of the more complex stuff and allows for these to be easier to interpret and clearer to understand.

2. Trim the data before the analysis

One of the steps that you should take form the very beginning is to trim up the data before you try to do any kind of analysis. This is so helpful in allowing you to have a better focus on what your analysis is doing. You have some freedom here because you can either go through and manually delete any of the variables that you don't need, or you can use the function for Define Variable Sets to help with this as well. Just make sure that before you do any of these two options though, make sure that you save the set of data to a separate set so that you don't end up with mistakes or missing data in the process.

3. Don't do the analysis on the master copy of the data

Another thing that we need to remember when we are doing some of our work here is that the analysis should never be done on the master, or the original, copy of the data. In general, there is nothing that you have to worry about when it comes to doing an analysis of all that data. This is due to the fact that it is really hard to mess up your data when you do perform one of these analyses. However, it is always best to err on the side of caution and never work with the master copy. If something does go wrong, then you have messed up your original copy and it is hard to get that back.

4. Don't base the hypothesis on a hunch

Forming a hypothesis is going to be one of the most important things that you do while working on data analysis. It helps you to go through all of the work that you want to do and actually find insights in all of that data. But the thing that we have to remember here is that the hypothesis needs to be based on facts and what we know for sure about the industry, rather than on a hunch. There is nothing that will be worse than trying to explain some kind of statistical anomaly that isn't really supported in the literature or the data that we have, or that may be found because of a random error. Keep your focus on the data at hand, and don't let those hunches get the best of you.

5. Accept that it is possible you won't find significance

It is possible, and something that you need to resign yourself too now, that you are maybe not going to find significance during this. And this means that we need to be able to devote some time to think about what all of this could mean to us. Preferably you are going to do this ahead of time. sometimes the best stories that come with the process of data analysis are going to be the ones about something didn't happen, even though we were expecting it, or finding that it didn't really pan out the way that you wanted.

6. Check your assumptions at the door before starting

Assumptions that are not backed by any data, or just backed by a hunch, are going to be the downfall to all of the work you are doing with the data analysis if you are not careful. You need to make sure that you check those assumptions at the door before you attempt to do anything to analyze the data that is available to you.

While this is sometimes a pain, and you may need to go through and remember to do this during the process, it is going to actually save you a lot of time and work when you are in the process of the analysis. This is due to the fact that violations of assumptions can sometimes make the outcomes of your data turn out a bit strange, and it can then lead you to try and explain out the findings in a manner that is not only strange but also not really valid in the process.

7. Select the analysis carefully

We need to make sure that before we get started on any of this process, that we choose the right analysis.

You may have to do some research on this before choosing. You can look it up online, read blogs, as a friend or a teacher, or even find a stats consultant. Do whatever steps it takes to make sure that, as you go through all of the data and work on your analysis, you are able to pick the appropriate analysis to help answer the question you have for the research.

Picking out the right analysis is so important from the very beginning of what you are trying to do. It ensures that the results you get are accurate and pertinent to what you are trying to do. And it can honestly save you as a programmer a lot of headaches in the process later on.

8. There is never a thing as bad results

Sometimes, it is easy to get frustrated by the results that you get. Maybe it is not showing you the answer that you were hoping for, or you just are not understanding the insight that is coming your way. Many business owners are going to fall into this category and will find that it is easy to just blame the data and will assume that it is giving them a bad result.

It can be hard to do this, but often the best approach is to just let the stats tell the story for your data. This is going to be easier said than done in some cases, it is going to actually save you some work, and ensure that you get the best results, compared to trying to rationalize it all out or finding out later that it was wrong. You also don't want to try and take the results and make them fit based on what your own notions about the result were in the beginning. Just let the data tell the story and see what is there to learn from.

9. Use syntax to help automate some of the repetitive analyses

This is going to be an important thing to work on because it helps to save you a lot of time, and will even be able to decrease the likelihood of any errors in the analysis. This is especially true when we compare it to running the analysis over and over again using the manual method. Try to save yourself some of the work and the hassle in the meantime, and use syntax or a prewritten code any time that you can.

10. Form a clear and specific hypothesis before you do the analysis

It is much easier for us to go through and test out one of our theories if we know ahead of time exactly what we would expect to happen, or what we don't expect to happen. This is going to also make it easier for us to prevent something that is known as the data fishing expeditions, which will carry with them a whole set of their own problems and complications.

Your goal is to not just look around and hope something just pops out. This would be nice, but you have way too much information to sort through to see this actually happening. Instead, you need to have a clear and concise, and even specific, hypothesis that you want to work with, and you need to stick with it. This helps to direct the search that you do and can make it easier to sift through all of that data.

Working on data analysis is one of the best things that you can do for your business. And when you combine it together with the Python language, you are certain to get the results that you want in no time. From forming the models to getting things to line up together, you will find that Python can help provide you with the tools and algorithms that you need to actually come up with the predictions. Following the tips above will help to make sure that you can get through all of that data, and work on accurate predictions, in less time than before.

Conclusion

Thank you for making it through to the end of *Python Data Analytics*, let's hope it was informative and able to provide you with all of the tools you need to achieve your goals whatever they may be.

The next stop is to start working through some of the steps that we talked about in this guidebook. We talked about what data science is all about, what the data analysis is, how to work with Big Data, and moved on to coding with the Python language so that we can work on some of the best data science libraries out there. With this in mind, we are able to work with creating our own data analysis to find the useful insights that are held inside.

Following the process of data analytics is simple, but it does take some time and usually, the algorithms and models need to be completed by a professional with the right education and experience. Understanding how this cycle works though can make a big difference in how we can work with it, and how well we know what is going on as we go through this process.

This whole process is going to start out with us gathering up the data that we would like to use when it comes to doing data analysis. Gathering the data from a lot of different sources, and gathering more data, ensures that we get the best picture of what is going on with our industry and with our business. After we have collected the information, especially if we are gathering it from a bunch of different sources, it is important for it to become organized and cleaned off, ensuring that we actually can use it.

At this point, the data is cleaned and organized and all of the missing values and duplicates are taken care of. And this leads us to work with creating a model and some algorithms that help us to analyze the data. Sometimes we can work with just one algorithm to do this, and other times we need to work with several. It all depends on the kind of data we are working with, the amount of data that we are working with, and what insights we would like to find with this.

In the end, we also need to be able to visualize what the data is telling us. It is not enough to just list it out on paper all of the time. While this can be a good extra step to work with, most of the time it is best if we can use some kind of visualization, like a chart or a graph, to help us really see the information and what it is sharing with us all in one place.

Working with a data analysis, especially when we can combine it together with the Python coding language, can do so many things when it comes to helping a business learn more about their customers, how to pick out the best products to develop and market, how to beat out the competition, and how to cut down on waste and improve the bottom line. When you are ready to work with Python data analytics and see these benefits and results in your own company, make sure to check out this guidebook to get started.

Description

Have you been collecting data on your industry, your product, or your customers, and now you are not sure what do to with it? Do you know that collecting this information is important and that there is likely to be some really valuable insights inside of that data, but you don't even know where to begin with extracting that data? Wouldn't it be nice to have a present model that could go through all of the information, and provide you with the answers, predictions, and insights?

This is exactly what data analytics is going to be able to help you out with! This is an amazing process that is simple to do, though it takes some time and some serious dedication to complete. The good news is, once you are able to put all of the parts together and see what is hidden in this data, it can provide you with so many benefits. From providing better customer service to beating out the competition and making decisions that are backed by data, you can't go wrong with adding data analytics into your business.

This guidebook is going to take some time to discuss what data analytics is all about, and why your business needs to have this process implemented into it as soon as possible. Some of the topics that we will discuss inside this guidebook to help put you on the fast track to seeing results with your data analysis include:

- What is a data analysis and why is it so important?
- Why do so many companies want to jump on board with everything a data analysis has to offer?
- A look at Big Data and where it fits in the picture
- What the Python coding language is all about, the benefits of using this coding language, and how it fits into the world of data science.
- Some of the best coding libraries that you can do to help with your own data analysis, including SciPy, NumPy, Pandas, and more!
- A few examples of coding that you can do to complete a data analysis
- Tips and tricks that can make your Python data analysis even better and more successful than before.

When you are ready to work with data analysis, and you want to use the Python coding language, with all of its great scientific and technical libraries to make it all happen, check out this guidebook and learn how to perform your very own Python Data Analytics today!